AF176232

The Love Of A Libra

Pia Krämer

The Love

Of A Libra

Pia Krämer

Bibliografische Information der Deutschen Nationalbibliothek:
Die Deutsche Nationalbibliothek verzeichnet diese Publikation
in der Deutschen Nationalbibliografie; detaillierte bibliografis-
che Daten sind im Internet über dnb.dnb.de abrufbar.

Text: © 2021 Pia Krämer

Umschlag: © 2021 Pia Krämer

Herstellung und Verlag: BoD - Books on Demand, Norderstedt

ISBN: 978-3-7543-3522-2

For all of those who try to find themselves in my words and for those who try to find something else in them and for those who only want to read these thoughts.

Just some thoughts

Just some experiments

Just something from me

For you <3

(The last three poems are a little older, but I
thought it would be a great idea to share them again
in this collection...)

The Tears Of The Moon

Hot tears running my face down.
Messy thoughts in my brain.
My head wears a heavy crown.
I'm the queen of the nightly rain.

The moon shines bright above.
The stars sparkle in the night.
Look me in my eyes, my love.
You might see everything's alright.

Tears of sadness belong to the past.
Tears of happiness surround me now.
I just hope these feelings will last.
Even if I don't know how.

But if you listen to the crying moon.
You'll understand it doesn't cry in pain.
Tears of joy will fall soon.
And I learn to enjoy the nightly rain.

The tears of the moon fall for the good.
But everybody expects the other side.
But just enjoy the falling flood.
And feel the joy and love and pride.

Be proud of what you've reached so far.
Think about the way you took.
Even if the past gave you a scar.
It is worth to take a look.

Look at the moon on a clear night.
The moon is proud of you.
It knows you are strong and you fight.
Tears of joy, they feel so true.

Hot tears running down my face.
I am happy and not sad anymore.
I float through the stars in space.
What is next for me in store?

(26.03.2020)

Lyrics Of The Flowers

Listen to this sweet melody.
Think about the words you hear.
These sounds and tones are here for you.
And the melody floats in your heart.

Feel the colors of the flowers.
Feel them through every single note.
It is there to let you feel.
Feelings that shine through your heart.

The sweet symphony flies through space.
And it comes back to earth.
Comes back to the flowers in my yard.
And fulfill the joy of my heart.

I love to hear the beauty of the flowers.
Tiny little shy blossoms of love.
The best thing you can hear on earth.
This is the most beautiful thing,
my heart.

(24.02.2020)

Small Things

Have you worried about life lastly?
Is anxiety hitting your heart?
Are the shadows of the past
Growing at your path?

But isn't it just the size
Which scares you?
Aren't these shadows just
Thoughts build up in your mind?

Realize there is so much more,
Hiding in these shadows.
Smaller things are on their way,
Trying to fill your empty heart.

They are beautiful and quiet,
Small and hardly seen.
They cheer you up,
As they always have been.

(26.03.2020)

Lullaby

And in the dark, I sing my song.
Silent voice you sound so calm.
You watch me feeling the beat in my heart.
And you fall asleep while watching.
I see your eyes flicker in your dreams
While I'm singing my sweet lullaby.
The music floats in the room
Fills the atmosphere around
And we both can't believe this is real.
Through these weird times of life
We lay here, in silence, and enjoy our
time.
And while you're dreaming of a better
world
I sing my sweet quiet lullaby about us
two.

(06.12.2020)

Wondering

I'm wondering about this world.

I'm wondering how a caterpillar uses metamorphosis to turn itself into the most beautiful tiny thing in the world. A butterfly with wings full of magic and secrets. I wish I could live through this kind of magic and begin to grow and be beautiful from the inside and the outside.

I'm wondering how a flower lives through different stages. From a small blossom to a great bloom. How its colors fade till the greyish colors fall into crunchy little pieces on the ground. And the flower lives until eternity and gives birth to its new self again and again.

I'm wondering how the moon travels in waves with the ocean. The flood of brightness shines through our hearts into our world. And even if it sometimes disappears it will always be there behind the clouds and thoughts.

I'm wondering how love can be so big. It hurts and weights so much. Like little rocks in our hearts that pull us deeper into our feelings and thoughts. We can't live without love but we aren't able to take this on our back on our own. We have

to love ourselves first to float through
the feelings with the biggest recognition
for it.

I'm wondering how I should live in this
world.
I'm not able to turn myself into something
more beautiful through magic. But I can
work on myself to live through my kind of
metamorphosis to create a better version
of myself like a butterfly.

I'm wondering how I should live in this
world.
I'm not able to live until eternity. But I
can rebirth myself into a tiny version of
myself with the love of my life. And
together we will fade into grey and loving
flowers.

I'm wondering how I should live in this
world.
I'm not able to disappear behind some
clouds. I'm always visual for the people
around me. But they may not notice my
complete existence and only after travel-
ing my way through the big ocean of life,
they will completely understand my impor-
tance.

I'm wondering how I should live in this
world.
I'm not able to love myself to the
fullest. It hurts that I cannot love my
mind and heart as it belongs to me. I'm
always one step ahead in my worries in my
mind and let my brain hurt me. But I can
and always will love you. And with your
love, I can try to love myself a little
more. And this leads to a bigger love for
you.

And through this all I'm creating my cir-
culation.
Circulation of developing, rebirthing,
living and dying, and loving.

And I'm wondering about this world and how
it all seems so logical.
But honestly, I can't explain.
I can just wonder about it.

(10.12.2020)

Skin

The hot water remembers me on your skin
Perfectly on mine and warming me and my
beating heart.
The hot water drops on the ground
Like the tears, I cried while laughing
The room is filling with fog and the
memory of our smiles
While we looked us in the eyes
Deep and full of shimmer
The cold of the room is heated up
A fever between us and our love
We can't stop and won't stop
It's like we only have each other
Are the only two people on this fucked up
earth
The hot air fills our lungs
And I try to catch a breath.
Giving you everything and my whole being
Like you give it to me
Electricity
and heat
And you
And
Me

(14.12.2020)

Lines

I follow the lines with my fingertips
Every little scar and stretchmark is so
perfect
A shape so soft and so cozy
I can't stop touching it

These lines form the perfect silhouette
A shadow in the dark
Just feeling every curve and every bone
Perfection on the wall, hardly seen

I feel your fingertips following the lines
The tickle leaves a smile on my face
You can't stop touching it
And you grin at me

And our lines melt together
As a perfect shape
Two shadows in the dark
Seen on the wall as there's just one

(17.12.2020)

Pure

It was pure
It was soft
It was slow
It was caring
It was light
It was a moment
It was silence
It was love
It was pure

(17.12.2020)

Coffee

There is something about drinking coffee
that makes it quite a thing for adults.
The hot cup with the caffeine
Milk or sugar added to it.
Drinking it in a hurry
Or if there's finally enough time.
Awakening and refreshing
Like you could activate your brain only
with this drink.
Saying "I can't survive my job without it"
And filling your body again and again with
this drug.
It's like when we grow up
We have to grab the coffee pot.
In the morning we define ourselves through
coffee
And in the evening through wine.
But honestly, we all adore great cocoa or
juice in the morning as well, isn't it?
And the only thing missing is the little
taste of bitterness that rests in the last
sip of coffee and makes me think that it's
like adult life.
Bitter and in a hurry.

(17.12.2020)

Wine

There is something about drinking wine
that makes it quite a thing for adults.
The great glass with the alcohol
Red or white, with ice added to it.
Drinking it in slow-motion
Or if there's time for partying.
Classy and socially
Like you could rest your brain only with
this drink.
Saying "I can't survive my job without it"
And filling your body again and again with
this drug.
It's like when we grow up
We have to grab the wine glass.
In the evening we define ourselves through
wine
And in the morning through coffee.
But honestly, we all adore a great coke or
lemonade in the evening as well, isn't it?
And the only thing missing is the little
taste of bitterness that rests in the last
sip of wine and makes me think that it's
like adult life.
Bitter and in slow-motion.

(17.12.2020)

The Look

The look
You gave me
On this picture
Pure love
And passion.

The look
I gave you
On this picture
Pure trust
And loving.

The look
Between us
A smile
With our eyes
And our hearts
Just the two of us
In this picture.

The look
We gave each other
Knowing quite well, it's just for us.

The look
A glance from eye to eye
From heart to heart
To you
My love.

(27.12.2020)

Body-Line

My body is my home
My home for my soul
My soul, my biggest good.

My body is flawless and beautiful
The truth I keep telling myself.
But sometimes, I only see the scars
On my body-line.

Scars are memories of my soul
Visible on my skin.
The parts that define my whole being
And the ground of the home I'm living in.

I see every body-line in the mirror
I see my whole being in front of me
Naked and clear.
I see the only home I will live in
forever.

My soul is kept in my body
My body is a fine line art
Every body-line is my home.

(27.12.2020)

Naked

I'm sitting on the ground
Naked
You can see every scar
Every part of my skin

Watching my body in the mirror
Naked
Makes me proud
Proud of what I see

I'm beautiful the way I am
Naked
Pretty and sexy
From every side I see

My skin is soft and shimmery
Naked
And without any protection
So vulnerable.

I see myself as perfect
Naked
Or with clothes
No matter what will happen

I step under the shower
Naked
Letting the water run over me
And my skin and hair

I feel free and good
Naked
In my very own body
I am the boss over it

This is just for me
Naked
And soft; my body is mine
But I might share it with you

And while you stare at my body
Naked
You will stare right in my soul
Naked

(30.12.2020)

Dance With Me

Dance with me
Like you try to catch me
for the very first time.
Wild and slow
Like we try to forget
The world around us.
Follow me with your eyes
And look at me
With passion.
This moment is a cage
For just the both of us
For our feelings and our hearts.
Dance around me
And try to touch me
And my soul.
And as we dance
Like strangers
Who become lovers
We make everybody jealous
Because we created a world
Just for the two of us.
A world
Just for our love.
Where we dance
And fall in love
Again and again.

(06.01.2021)

Pillow

I lay on you
Like you're my pillow.
Warming us in these cold times.
You hold me tight
Like you are afraid of losing me
During these cold and heavy times.
I lay my head on your shoulder
And my whole weight is carried by your
body.
Like a pillow
You are my comfort zone.
I'm trying not to move
Cause I'm afraid
this moment would disappear.
And during this cold January
And this heavy time
I feel so blessed and safe
Having you
My person
Who I can lay on
Where I can let me fall.

(06.01.2021)

Finally Found Her

You didn't know
I heard you
That night
You said
'I finally found her'
Saying my name
Sounding so thankful
And glad
And I smiled
With my whole heart.
And you didn't know
I heard you
That night
You called me
Your woman
Like I'm already yours
Forever and until time
And I smiled
With my whole heart
And knew
You're mine

(10.01.2021)

Mirror

Mirrors show us the truth
Bittersweet
But this is just reality
There in front of me
In this mirror.
It shows my past
My present
My future
Just me.
Every line and scar
What made me cry
What kept me alive.
Undressing
Still looking in the mirror
Just feeling my soul in this body
Pulsing alive in my veins.
I am proud of what I see
Because it is the truth.
And aren't we all craving after it
After the naked and ugly truth.
And here I am…
True
Naked
Me
Standing
Staring
In the mirror
A glass that shows
I'm alive.

(13.01.2021)

Silence

Thunder
Lightning
Raining through the night
We can hear every drop
This is what we call our silence.
The cold nights around us
But we are in the warm cloud of our flat
Feeling the silence
Sometimes loud
Sometimes quiet
Heart and heart
Beating like they want to be heard
But the only thing we want to hear
Is this silence around us
Loud
Deaf
Breath

(14.01.2021)

Kiss My Ass

I do not belong in the kitchen
I belong into a boss office
While you see me fly above
Please, just kiss my ass.

(17.01.2021)

Art

I walk through a museum.
A museum of mine.
I look around and see him.
He stands with others in a line.
All of them try to catch
The art I call my own.
They think it's all a match,
A game to win every bone.
To win my art, my everything.
To be a chaser of my string.
But don't touch the art, be strict,
It's precious and rare and perfect.
This art is everything but mine
The body I try to keep so safe,
And he tries to catch this line
And be an owner of my art, unsafe.
Every woman is perfect like I am.
Not every man is like this.
But we are art; get this, goddamn!
And the truth hurts, the truth it is:
That male break art
Touch it without permission.
That female is a mortician
Of the pieces of her art.
Her body is a soul, a machine, a grave.
We are, we create and we bury.
So don't pretend like you're so brave
To ruin this museum of glory.

(17.01.2021)

Dreaming Dreams

I'm just dreaming dreams
But they feel so good
Even if reality is more real
The feelings are the same.
Touching and kissing
Laughing and crying
Is it you or someone else
I can't see or
Can't decide.
You make me happy
But the dreams as well.
I enjoy these feelings
I fall for these adventures.
But in the end
I'm here in reality
Here for everyone who's real.
In the end
I'm only dreaming dreams.

(26.01.2021)

WTF

What the fuck?
What went wrong?
What is the fucking problem?
What do you want from me?
What the hell do you try to tell me?
Tell them, I am a machine.
Tell them, I am stronger.
Tell them, I am a fucking queen.
Tell them, I am here for winning.
Tell them, I am a nightmare and a dream.
Fuck you, the world belongs to me.
Fuck you, my thoughts are important.
Fuck you, I am a woman, what now?
Fuck you, I don't care what you think
'bout me.
Fuck you, listen to me, don't try to
change me.
WTF?
With my whole heart
Take my anger
Feel free to think about it.

(27.01.2020)

Bestie

I miss you so bad.
I miss you so bad.
So so bad.
I miss your smell.
I miss your big paws.
I miss your fur.
Your black hairs,
Everywhere
In the tiniest corner
Of the house.
I miss your dark bark.
I miss your eyes
Following me around
Every step I take
No matter where.
I miss you waving
Happily
Exciting
A little cold wind.
I miss your weight on me
When you lay in my lap
Like you're a puppy again.
I miss you like crazy
My best friend
The true love of my life.
I miss how your paws
Left a footstep in my heart
With every day
I woke up
The first thing
Was greeting you.

Were you greeting me.
I miss every walk
Even if we both were lazy
Sometimes.
I miss you.
So so bad
I miss you so bad.
I miss you so bad.

(31.01.2021)

Vinyl

Black.
Circles.
Spinning around.
Listening to the sounds.
The past whispers to me
Through the speakers.
I am moving from side to side.
The skirt swirls around.
The dust lays on the black surface
And I can hear a little crack in the
sound.
The candles give me a little light.
I can barely see
But I can feel it all.
It floats through my veins
And comes out of my mouth
A silent voice
Singing to all the one-hit wonders.
The needle stops and interrupts me.
I smile
But my eyes are disappointed.
The short trip is over.
Back in reality
No music around.
The only thing left
A little rustle
While spinning around.
The circles.
Something black.

(02.02.2021)

Paris

It's been a while.
It was a different time.
Years ago.
The fog lays on the old streets.
A slightly shimmer through the heavy
clouds
I can barely imagine the sun behind.

The steel above me is breathtaking
And still something so familiar.
I feel like I'm a part of a postcard.
Standing underneath.
A stranger in this city.
The old streets offer me their magic
And I try to catch it.

Before, I was shocked.
Rubbish, poverty, people.
All at the same place.
The spotlight has its specific place
In this city which tries to hide its prob-
lems
And reality.

Dans la Champs-Élysées
I see a bride.
Standing in the middle of the street
Keeping her most special day in a photo-
graph.
The next sightseeing stop in the back-
ground

But on the side
People hush from store to store.
Not interested in this beautiful view.

We drive over a place
Hotels around us, surrounded by the fog.
A famous one once left this building
Never came back.
A lady to die.
Sad and unbelievable.
A woman, as beautiful as this city.

What else is there to tell
About a city like this?
Another woman,
Smiling in secret,
Unfortunately,
I did not see.

I was young
Lost in the beauty of this city.
But still aware of what was hidden behind,
Behind this golden curtain.
Between history lays homeless.
Buildings reaching for the sky
Where they try to cover what's hopeless
In a city like Paris.

(02.02.2021)

Rome

Hush from place to place.
Ancient buildings.
I can't decide where to look.
The heat is burning down on me
As I try to choose my first destination.
Colors like sepia
I jumped directly into this history book.

Years ago they fought for freedom
Today we fight for tickets.
To get inside,
where some just wanted to escape.
Every step feels unreal...

The forum is so beautiful.
I feel like a historian,
like an archaeologist,
like Indiana Jones.
A garden, a destroyed city, a grave.

And suddenly,
Dark sky, heavy clouds,
summer rain falls on my skin.
Cooling down this hot atmosphere.
But the rain can't stop us.

Our journey continues.
Money for luck,
What kind of paradox thought.
Don't look behind your coins.
But just here or also in reality?

Buildings, cold stone, hot rain.
People in excitement.
The smell of pizza is combined with
emissions.
Motorola, musica, magia.

Steps to Spain.
Or at least something like that.
A great view of the plaza and the streets.
And the last place makes me feel so small.
But the surrounding is small as well,
belonging to god, a religious country.

Old.
Ancient.
Interesting.
Rome.

(02.02.2021)

Barcelona

I think about colors.
I think about the sun.
I think about fruits.
I think about flowers.

I see the sun and the blue sky.
I see the airplanes and busses.
I see the little cafes and stores.
I see some great buildings, as I walk by.

I smell the sun blocker on my skin.
I smell the food and fruits around.
I smell the cars and air, not clear any-
more.
I smell the people, black, white, big,
thin.

I walk to the top of the mountain.
I walk through a park, colors around.
I walk to collect a new adventure.
I walk to see a view, the greatest I can
imagine.

I feel this fire for this city.
I feel an inspiring thought in these
streets.
I feel a muse growing in me.
I feel Barcelona beating in my heart.

(02.02.2021)

Please...

Please, just love yourself more.

Please, just believe in yourself more.

Please, be kind to your skin.

Please, keep a smile on your face.

Please, realize what made you so far.

Please, don't hurt your soul so bad.

Please, just let me show you how beautiful
you are.

Please, love your mindset, love your opin-
ion.

Please, just see that's how you are.

Please, I want you to see your clear
heart.

Please, stay!

(02.02.2021)

Window Walk

Shimmer on the glass.
Skin so soft and fine.
A woman made with class.
Her shadow, a thin line.
She stands in her bedroom.
Til kept in her dreams.
Still looking for the perfect groom,
But she doesn't need, and has no scheme.
Just loves what amazes her,
and adores the beauty in the world.
She crosses her room, goes there,
goes here, to take her bra, white pearled.
Her clothes seem pure and clean,
but her heart is colored and
like her black dress, like a queen,
of night, she's mysteriously glorious.
Walking every day around,
like a goddess who observes,
her people on the streets around.
She shows her body, being, curves.
The window keeps her privacy
and does not allow to come closer
to keep her conscious, no anxiety,
to love her body, to be just her.
No shame, no touching, no scare,
just love, acceptance, she's so rare.

And through this window
everybody can see her,
how she walks and shows
her beauty and strength.

(02.02.2021)

The Shore

At the end of the world
there's a shore.
Stony, cold, desolate,
alone, scary, dark.
The water is loud,
I can't hear my own thoughts.
The darkness is deep,
only the waves light it up a little.
I can't see.
Where does the journey continue?
Is there still a chance?
Is there still a 'going on'?
The shore is loud,
and frightening.
Can I survive
or had I already lived
enough?

(02.02.2021)

Strength

The dust swirls around
Footsteps heavy on the ground
A look in the new direction
Heart beats loud and fast
The body strong and big
Big in its attendance
Big in its thoughts
Keep real
Stay there
Take your strength
Use it kind
Use it wise

(02.02.2021)

Steering Wheel

Behind the steering wheel
I see the lights reflecting on the
streets.
Red and white
In the mirror of the falling rain.
The speed limit stops me
And my thoughts
In this box made out of metal.
I feel the leather under the tips of my
fingers.
I can slightly smell the scent of fuel.
The curves lead me to another place
A new town I'd like to reach.
And as I drive through the night
I hear my thoughts whisper in my mind.
The darkness and the speed
Let me become emotional
I feel so tiny in the world.
The moon follows me on my road
And stays by my side.
The wheels hit the ground
and get me where I belong to be.
And behind my steering wheel
I feel safe.

(03.02.2021)

Blank Page

I write my thoughts
On my naked skin
With black ink
From the bottom of my heart.
This small body
A blank page
Craving for the right words to say.
Every inch of my skin
Feels nothing without a dream
Without a thought
From the depth.
Take the ink and just start writing
Let out what you want to say
Feel free to tell the world
What you're hiding inside.
My skin is a blank page.
Soft and white.
The cage of my thoughts
And the page for my words.

(10.02.2021)

More

Tell me more about where you're from.
Tell me more about your thoughts.
What are your issues?
What are your dreams?
I want to understand your beautiful being.
Living so weightless in this heavy world.
But maybe this is just what you allow to
see.
I want to feel what you have to carry
I want to see the tears you hide so deep.
Tell me more about you and your past.
Tell me more and more and more.
I will follow every move of your lips
Until they form the words I try to catch
I try to understand.
To understand you.
To understand more.

(17.02.2021)

Blind

You can't see
It is dark
You close your eyes
You try to ignore
Pretend like you can't see.
You're blind to see.
You're blind to feel.
Don't allow the truth.
Don't allow the pain.
Issues around you
Unable to see.
Look at it.
See how it hurts.
See what you've done.
Feel the pain.
Feel the truth.
Feel it
Through the blind.

(18.02.2021)

My Polaroid

I keep this polaroid
Close to my heart.
I remember this evening
With every look on it.
I love these colors
I love this look.
A night to remember
A night to feel.
To feel this depth
In both our eyes.
To feel the light
Of the lightning of the camera.
This camera kept my perfect moment.
My whole world and my whole love.
This polaroid is like a promise.
The promise to keep this in my heart.
To keep you in my heart.
To keep the memory in my heart.
I want this polaroid in a big frame
To let everybody see.
But honestly,
The feeling works best,
In this small frame,
Of the polaroid.

(18.02.2021)

Behind My Blue Eyes

Where my story lies.
Behind this blue shimmery look
You can read me like an open book.
Through the blue, and through the dark
You can see my past, with every part.

Look me in my eyes
Where my whole being lies.
Please, just see the glance,
I want to catch your pretty face.
Give my blue blue eyes the chance
To also see what is really the case.

My blue eyes full of feeling
Full of loss and healing.
The story behind is chaotic,
Past, present, future, poetic,
Fantastic, crazy, but true.
But see and I may show you.

Behind my blue eyes
Where my heart and my soul lies.
Caring and vulnerable, loving.
Warming and mad, doubtful.
Feelings that belong to the living.
That belongs to me. Delightful

How life can be seen only
Through eyes, together, but lonely.
The blue, an ocean of tears
And the cold of my fears.
Meet my true self, it lies
Behind my blue eyes.

(19.02.2021)

Enjoyable Whisper

I whisper a kiss in your ear
Slowly filling the silence
With a slight laugh
Enjoying the little moment
Every inch of my skin feels love
And my mind falls
Through the clouds of my thoughts
The music floats in my heart
The feelings fill my lungs
I breathe a whisper on your cheek
And I let it all fly through the room
Joy and freedom of my thoughts
Silent and slightly felt
We feel the enjoyable whisper
Of life and love

(19.02.2021)

The Love Of A Libra

I am a little crazy and a little moody,
I already know, but I'm true.
My behavior is sometimes strange
And I am not patient with myself.
But you will gain my patience
You will gain my love, my heart.
I believe in chaos and harmony.
I think every mind has its fantasy.
A fantasy that is always real
And, more important, important.
Tolerance, acceptance, respect.
I will fight for your right, after mine.
A look in the stars and space
Trying to gaze me in between.
They twinkle in my blue eyes as a shadow.
And my thoughts float between every orbit.
I love these silent nights
I adore every tiny light above me.
My mind cares for me,
But for everybody else before.
I think every human is perfect in his own
way.
No matter which color or race.
Just like flowers, everyone is beautiful
Especially because of their differences.
Take my love. This pure love.
I do not expect anything in return.
But I would grow,
With more love for me.
But the love of me is so big.
The love of a libra is huge.

(19.02.2021)

The Night I Wore Stars

There is a night
I remember
Light and applause.
Memories and adventures.
The end and the beginning.
A night to remember.
I feel the blue material
Dancing with my skin.
The memory of the sun
Kissed my skin and hair.
I can't realize
This moment.
My top is blue
Like the night
Around me.
The glitter is flirting
With every spotlight around.
The music stops
as I leave this stage
And step into the last night
In this building.
And in this night
The glitter catches the light of the
stars.
I dance with them
In a dark and smoky room.
The smell of the smoke
Takes over the smell of this adventure.
This night my future has started.
This night I looked in my deepest memory.
This night I wore stars.

(19.02.2021)

Luna's Smile

At this night
We just might
Be two small parts
Of the world's arts.
The art of humans
Oceans,
Land.
We both stand
On this holy ground.
And we just found
That we are wonders.
The sky, lightning, thunders,
Stars and clouds, and
Suddenly luna comes above the land.
We smile at the sky,
We can't realize it all, but we try.
We are too small for it all,
We just fly and let us fall,
Through this big world around.
And the only thing we found
Is that someone is watching us.
Someone stares silently at us.
It takes care of you and me,
Luna stops and see,
How we try to understand,
What's around, the great big land.
Luna smiles at us so wonderful,
We stare back, but cannot understand.

(20.02.2021)

Two Glasses Of White Wine

We sat there in silence
And the glasses were filled
We held them between thin fingers
And let the liquid float through our
throat.
I taste the fine line of wine on my lips
And I can see the drops running down the
glass.
The bottle on the ground
Cold and already nearly emptied.
The room was filled with happiness
But also with memories.
Just a few nights for us
And just some glasses of wine
From time to time.
And the wine is like a glue
For the society in this small room.
I believe we would have nothing in common
If it wasn't the alcohol in our veins.
We sit here in silence
With two glasses of wine
And no topic to talk about.

(22.02.2021)

Period

You read correctly
I am going to talk
About the big secret
That everybody knows.
It's natural, it's real
I think no human doesn't know.
But, how could I even thought,
It would be okay to talk about.
Shame on me!
What the hell am I talking about?
But honestly,
Listen to me.
This is the reality.
This is the truth.
I can't understand
Why everybody shuts up
Instead of shouting out the truth.
Women listen,
Don't be ashamed.
Talk about it,
Tell everybody
It's reality, it's pain, it's a part of
us.
Every month I try to hide
That I am a woman
That I am who I am.
But why should I?
It's nature and my life.
I am proud to be a girl, woman, female,
wife.

(22.02.2021)

You Light And Me

And nothing in between

(23.02.2021)

Eclipse

Sometimes the darkness overcomes me.
And I can't feel, can't love, can't see.
Everything feels so unconscious.
And nothing feels so glorious.
It's like a black dot comes over my sun,
And I can't move, can't live, can't run.

(23.02.2021)

Rest In Peace

Every regret and every lost moment.
We buried all the opportunities
We buried it all, because of what?
Shyness and low self-esteem?
Society made us feel weak
It made us feel wrong
We bury our chances and adventures
We never experienced or enjoyed it.
The grave is full of moments,
we might have lived through.
But we weren't meant to be, to have it
all.

(24.02.2021)

Flames In The Sky

The sky is burning
The fire is falling
The earth moves slowly
And I stand in the middle
I stare at the flames above me
Still trying to not lose hope
I stay strong and I try to heal
Even if everything around struggles
The sky burns and I can feel the heat on
my skin
The stars are falling and burning
And they won't come back.
They end and fall and burn
And we cry
Cause we know
We could have done better.

(05.03.2021)

Nudity

We were born naked
Our soul isn't wrapped in clothes
We are free and naked and pure.
Our comfort zone should be our body
Our home and soul place.
Skin soft, lips wet, hair with shimmer
Nothing else around.

(07.03.2021)

The Rose

The rose
The rose
She grows
She grows

Her head
Full of love
And passion
Red and soft

Her thorns
Pain and worries
It hurts
She's hurt

Green and long
Like hope
And happiness
And positivity

Every leaf
Individual
Will go
Comes back

The rose
She grows
The love
She grows

(09.03.2021)

Home

I will call several places my home.
There are people, places, feelings.
My house with every memory
Of childhood and growth.
My family with every hug
And warming smiles.
My island with the wind,
The sea, nature.
My love with every high and low
With heart and soul.
I call a lot my home.
When my heart feels warm
And the sun shines through
I feel safe and comfortable
And I feel home.

(10.03.2021)

iPhone Camera

We scroll.
We like.
We enjoy
Our deepest
Moments through.
No eyes
Needed anymore.
Videos, photos
Replace dreams.
Lightning on,
Smile on.
A moment,
Just one
To realize
We are blind.

(10.03.2021)

Midnight Smoke

The cigarette is lightened up.
I am standing on the street
Darkness around me.
Far away a little light from a street lamp
And a little whisper from the wind.
I feel the cold air on my skin
And the warm smoke in my lungs.
I stare above.
Stars surround me.
I am just a little part of this endless
universe.
Far away I can hear a car
driving through the night.
I hold the cigarette between my teeth
I let the smoke, just a little, in my
mouth,
My throat, my lungs
The rest floats into the midnight sky.
My thoughts are somewhere in between the
stars
I can't reach them.
I try to feel my heart beating in my
chest.
The smoke takes my thoughts and feelings
And let them disappear in the air
And in the night.
The midnight smoke washes my mind out
Makes it free
And empty.

(11.03.2021)

The Islander

My heart is buried
Deep under the white sand
Where the water hits the land
And my soul is kept
Within the wind and the clouds
White and always present.
And my thoughts are there
Between the fields and nature
In peace and alone.
I am an islander
My heart beats for this place
I miss being buried
I miss being kept
I miss being there.
Years ago my little feet in the sand
My light hair in the wind
Wild and free
And my mind so free and pure.
I want to be a child again
I want it so bad
I want to be the islander again.
This is where I want to be.
I know deep inside
I am an islander.

(11.03.2021)

Fortune-Teller

I met a fortune-teller last night.
She told me about my future.
She saw it bright and clear.
But she was worried a little.
I wasn't sure if I wanted to know.
I thought I could be afraid
Of life or future.
She held my hand
And looked me in my eyes
And whispered
"You have to realize who's true.
People are bad. People are liars.
Your kind heart will be hurt"
And I asked myself:
Who would stab me behind my back?
But then I realized
It was always somebody else.
I already saw them
They already hurt me.
I knew I should learn more
About who should share my path
Who should leave my story
Who already did it years ago
Who is here to heal me forever.
The fortune-teller smiled at me
She knew I would choose the right way
She knew I would recognize the people.
But she still was worried
She was worried if I could hurt people
By being too honest and being too real
By being too kind and being too pure.

I learned people will be bad
But I forgot that I might be too good.

(11.03.2021)

The Bird On The Branch

The bird on the branch
He saw it all
He saw the pain and worries of us all.
He sat there day by day.
No reason to fly, no reason to stay.
Wondering where God might be
Wondering if he could see
What went wrong and destroyed us
How we shout and cry, discuss.
The bird holds his wings up high
But still not tries to fly
He uses them as protection
For his kind heart, a reflection
Of what's lost in the world here
And what he tries to find again there.
The bird there on the big tree
Made of love and happiness and so free
He saw the problems of us all
He saw it all
He worried about our future
And our hearts.

(11.03.2021)

Dots And Lines

A dot. A line.
Thin. And fine.
Words. Like whisper.
Silence. Cry.
Write. And read.
The dot. The line.
Thin paper. Words so fine.

(12.03.2021)

Tulips In My Bed

One for love
One for childhood
Both for happiness
I lay on my bed
Stare at the wall
Grin from heart to soul
See the flowers around
I smell their scent
I remember my story
Colors full of emotions
Buy me some
I buy myself all.
I take them with me
Every day
And I put the roses in a place
Where everyone can see them
But the tulips are for me
I take them with me
I take them to my bed
Hoping for a dream about my childhood
In colors
In happiness

(12.03.2021)

Maybe I'm Finally A Butterfly

Maybe. Yes maybe. I survived.
I spread my wings. One after another.
And I realize I'm back at life.
I stretch my body and feel everything.
Leaving my cocoon felt so good.
I left my comfort zone. I'm free.
Happiness fills my body. From head to toe.
I can see the sun on my body
And I feel the warmth floating through my
veins.
I am maybe; yes maybe, a new person
Or maybe the old with a new mindset.
I maybe; yes maybe, lost my worries
And anxiety and despair and fear.
I developed myself, left some people be-
hind
And I left a lot of issues behind
I lost weight and problems and
Maybe I'm finally a butterfly
Flying through life
Happy
Enjoying
Everything.

(12.03.2021)

The Purest Emotion

```
It's more than love
It's more than a word
Nothing to describe this
It's the purest emotion
It's nothing and everything
I can't imagine a world without
Forever
Mom, I love you.

(13.03.2021)
```

Just Do

Sing every line of the song
Wrong
Just get this tattoo on your skin
So thin

Close your eyes and feel the world
Just do anything you love

Dance to every song you hear
With no fear
Just drink that drink and eat this cake
Do and make

Close your eyes and feel the world
Just do anything you love

Travel the world, get on that plane
Or the train
Just love with passion and your whole
Soul

Close your eyes and feel the world
Just do anything you love
Because it's all for you

(13.03.2021)

My Little Star

I would do anything for you
I would get every star from the sky for
you
I would kick everyone's ass for you
I would write every love story for you
I would drive a thousand miles for you
You are my little star
My biggest love

(13.03.2021)

Happy Hour

It's the last hour of the day
The light is dimmed
The sky is black
Light dots represent the stars
Around us nothing like love
And fun and happiness
We take a sip of our drink
And let the emotions float through us
Our veins are filled with the thought of
tomorrow
And our true selves and our confidence
We no longer hide that we are stronger
We are better and we are happier
It's the happy hour
It's our last step
It's our final destination
Into a poetic and enjoyable life
It's the great final
For our heart and soul
And our pure love
And kindness.
In our head applause
For what we've reached so far
And at this moment
We know
We are true
And we are perfect
Exactly how we are
And how we are born
And how we will die
With a smile on our face

And a thankful thought
About our life
And our love
The love of a libra
Endless

(13.03.2021)

Magic Moment

The magic moments
Are the times,
When you can see
The sun and the
Moon both shining!

(19.07.2016)

Different

Do not ignore!
I am different too!
For a good life!
For a great world!
Everybody is different!
Red, white, black, or brown?
English, German, African, French?
No matter where you are from!
Twinkle and show who you are!

(28.07.2016)

Dream

Fly away to the stars,
Forget all problems and all wars.
In the ocean full of dreams.

We'll find out everything,
The waves slowly begin to sing.
In the ocean full of dreams.

Think about the way you take.
Don't dream your life - do and make.
In the ocean full of dreams.

Every shimmer, every way.
Swim in the sea, to the bay.
In the ocean full of dreams.

(25.10.2016)

Love.

Pia Krämer

Pia Krämer

wurde 1999 in Recklinghausen geboren und lebt seit ihrem 2. Lebensjahr im oberbergischen Wiehl. Nach dem Abitur 2018 begann sie ein Lehramtsstudium an der Universität in Siegen.

Seit ihrer Kindheit schreibt sie schon Geschichten und hat 2020 ihren ersten Jugendroman *Wolfsaugen* fertiggestellt. Daneben schreibt sie auch Kinderbücher, Kurzgeschichten und deutsch- sowie englischsprachige Gedichte. 2021 wagte sie den Schritt und ging ins Self-Publishing.

Auf Instagram ist sie unter @piakraemer29 zu finden.

Pia Krämer was born in 1999. She is studying to be a teacher at the University of Siegen. She writes books for children and teenagers, but also short stories and German and English poems. In 2021, she published her first German novel for teenagers as a Selfpublisher.

Instagram: @piakraemer29